city poems

mia kang

ignitionpress

To Cam Scott, my love and gratitude are endless.

First published in 2020
by **ignition**press
Oxford Brookes Poetry Centre
Oxford Brookes University
OX3 0BP

© Mia Kang 2020

Cover design: Flora Hands, Carline Creative

A CIP record for this book is available from the British Library

ISBN 978-1-9161328-2-5

Contents

…without books love is just the signifier!
Bernadette Mayer

Cam, Apart, September 9, 2019

My god,
they are not going to touch each other.

—Sharon Olds

On the pier we watched
golf balls fly inside the oversized cage.

You liked the sound.
You like the sound

of the J train overhead
outside the Korean restaurant

where I first made you
blush about your book

coming out this week.
I could see you under yourself

as if under dark, spinning
into chainlink.

I knew I could not
keep you

unless I stayed
shattered by your star

wrote to you only
until the end,

Canadian fool
full of lines and Lacanian conceits.

Look at you now—
far away, closer than ever.

New Haven, August 8, 2017

I lack the libido to write city poems,
writes Cam, and I

now lack the city
and its popular synecdoches:

straphangers, manholes
grids and bridges.

I despise Whitman
and Brooklyn, and gatherings

of euphonic youngthings
about whose oratorios

he and I would then
dash to pieces

our two heads, ambulatory
and intransitive,

standing on the pier
in the freezing cold

on Halloween
every night of the year,

the city a ship or a crazy castle
across this or that river, dark

moving line we mark
with pleasure

objecting indirectly
and hardly holding hands.

Europe Swelters Under a Heat Wave Called 'Lucifer'

Temperatures in parts of the Continent have soared to record highs, causing at least two deaths, kindling wildfires and driving tempers through the roof.
—*The New York Times*, August 6, 2017

Meteorologists agree—tempers and temperatures
talk to each other. Avoid love
in the summer; you might die of heat exhaustion. Avoid
love in the winter; it could leave you cold. Is our relief

in naming things simply the smallest
form of action, or is it just so satisfying to say the name
Lucifer? When we talk about the wolf, he stands
behind the door. Speaking of the king of Rome,

through the door he appears. *Lupus in fabula!*
a good Roman exclaims, when an object of conversation
arrives on the scene. Speak of the dog, ready
the stick. Poor sufferers—with language as cane

to condition our air, we're definitively
going to the canines. If excessive summer
can cause you to curse, can kill the elderly
expiring alone, doesn't some part

of you wish for a wildfire? I dream Lucifer
will approach me in my modern life
in this American town
and retrieve from me every secret heat:

lapsed citizen, attempering intemperately, descending
into hell the way a body sinks
into a bubble bath. Mention the lion, he eats you.
I couldn't help but call it love.

Qui transtulit sustinet

I lack the libido to write city poems
writes Cam, and I am a child again

sad and afraid, staring
at the stripes the streetlights make

through the blinds. *This is neither*
a time nor a place

writes Ben, and I am a woman
in bed with a stranger, awake in a town

that isn't home. Sleeping
isn't losing, but there is a risk

in not savoring this
wrongness. I left home

as a child and went
where I found it. When I left

again, I could see ahead,
but important organs

quivered back in Brooklyn. What is
he to me? What is one love

or another, how do they
talk to each other

the way poems do, trying to match
word for moment? It's my lover

asleep beside me
and my dearest counterpart who

is not. It's not the city
poem at stake, but the maudlin college

town homesickness, wandering leafy
Victorian blocks

and trying to remember
the fantasy version. *Some other*

place, some / other time not this
one, writes Robert, and he could

have meant New Haven
in August, or New York

in the body as it fights
the fall. It isn't libido

lacking here, nor any skyline
disappearing. All my language

is up for grabs. I wait
for the scaffolding to hold me.

America in Love, with Canada (I)

I imagine winning, then I think of
the distance it will take me
to get to you.

When I win, I'll be
on a train, on the telephone to you
moving toward what, once arrived upon,

will feel as if it must have passed
me, going in the other direction.
It's easy to say you're a stand-in

for that original, absented figure,
but it's also easy
to say no, this is it, this is

the one I'll marry
so he can work legally
in this country, at that bookstore

that I like, which has fed me
more than books in having
landed you in my city, which I then

left; and whose premises are, by the way,
our scene of imagined encounter, deflated
and full of promise, after I win.

Ekphrastic: Internet Photo of Cam Taking Off His Shirt, Accompanying Interview with Kevin Killian (or Phrases K to C, the Dick is on the Wall)

[No one knows but me
now I've ruined it
and it isn't true]

the dear heart on torso
lower left, but who's counting

who's in the know
but me, I count
now I've lost my place

I have no place
tattooing your name in my poems

in the shape of a heart
sad read trace
I want to come

to, as a person who can
know something

without needing to know
don't mask, don't yell
but the red

heart draws the I
where you opened it once

on the street and
I put a hand to you, to keep you
there where I had no

knowledge
the fantasy is of sleeping

we do it together
and when you wake we say
I don't know what to do

repeatedly
I am always seeing

your shoulder blades under the shirt
I am between them
you are not undressed

by a photo, poem, or dialogue
I learn so much from the cock on the wall

as if I could put you
to bed by citation
hey, I don't want you

in my bed anyway
[no one knows but me

now I've ruined it
and it isn't true]
I know better

looking at the photo
than I do in the bed

enough to make the call
is that enough, the border of skin
showing above the waistband

or the hand splayed
all I can see is the heart

despite the cock
the blue painter's tape
I know how you stand

I'd know you anywhere
getting nowhere

or getting there
the action sequence
damn the denouement

when you rise to relieve yourself
I make the coffee

why are you lifting your hands
the cock is drawn
the shirt stays on

there's no sex in this picture
no sex in my poems

there is no sex
there is no such thing as no sex
I'm doing it right now

and you know it
no one knows but me

[it isn't true
but I have ruined it]
or would, or fear I would, or fear I have

by way of the thing
the red needle

how can I decide if I want one
what will time do to the skin
i.e. how much will it reveal

if we develop the strip
if I get things started

let me enumerate
details for the audience
which only I know

no, no audience
is wholly unknown or wholly anonymous

I'm afraid of knowing others
I'm afraid of you
knowing others, loving others

that's why I put the red on
the skin, protesting

I learn so much from the cocked wrist
it tells me what I notice
noticing that thumb hooked

under the t-shirt, pulled like a tent
hiding the head

facing the wall
except when you look at me
I watch your head cock

I'm in your chest
that no one sees

due to modesty or ritual
shame, same thing
I don't decide

because of the heart, I keep
looking at it

you lean into one hip
your forearms are crossed
above your head

who goes there, I go
too far maybe, I don't know

how to not kiss you
but I don't
it might ruin the photo

the wrists almost kiss
in the image, the shoulder

blades move toward each other
it could happen
any time now, no one knows

but me how long I've waited
I'm lying, I forestalled

or foreshortened
to try to get some perspective
did it work, ha

no one loves like this
everyone loves like this

and it isn't true

Love is Not Uncomplicated

But whom do you text when John Ashbery dies—
that's how you know whom you love.

I'd like to think so
since someone else texted me.

I joined Twitter or something.
Over drinks, I heard the girl say

"When I was phone banking for Bernie Sanders"
and I left the room.

The graduate students wanted to know
if I would join the union

if I would get organized. I would
if it would help me get hired.

I dream of becoming John Ashbery,
dream a beautiful house

full of art and sounds of marriage.
Among the other art historians

I passed around the anthology
and everyone read a poem

because of you, John Ashbery, your death
and the way America promises

to outmode its modernisms
to detract its detractors

and to school us so well
in the politics of the circle.

The Poet Refreshes Her Home Page

I lack the libido to write
city poems, writes Cam, and my gmail

emboldens in delight. I curse the wire
-lessness that tethers us, nervous

system striking keys, body
beating our sick heart in time

to post-move type. I ruined my mascara
reading your manuscript. I applied the stuff

to walk around the Green, buy flowers
and a vase, then spent an hour

aborting stems all over the kitchen.
The arrangement doesn't suit me

no matter how I turn it. See?
I'll even imitate your voice

just to hear it. If it were me, I'd double
down on anaphora now: "I'll even"

fill in the blank until
the sudden turn, and scene. Words

are without wires, though not innocently so.
You stole my line, I said it too, but I still had to go.

Graduate Student, Age 27, with a History of Sexual Harassment by Professors and Employers, Attends a Poetry Reading Four Days After the Tax Heist, Falling for a Man Who Isn't Her Lover, Temperature 54° F, New Haven, CT, December 5, 2017

Because the edges don't obtain
in the would-be winter

something in me
goes the way of the world

climbing at a normal pace
toward a figure on the stairs

something in me
gets everywhere

Univers/ity Poetics

I feel I must load everything into the upper register
My friends, I have been getting louder

In coming from the city to the enclave
I have learned about insignia

I have told ten undergraduates
To properly signpost their topic sentences

For which I was paid
Twenty-three dollars an hour

I have said I have seen the signs
And therefore, must turn away

Onto a new path, fearing
A new path is never possible

I feel I have shouted for a rescue party
But the canary keeps dying inside

I have transcribed the error of my ways
Making mistake a mantra

I feel I must signpost entitlement
In the title of the poem, naming

What I have not named before
My friends, how much have I left

To the text, what is my
Position or argument, or are those

Coterminous, but didn't identity
Politics fail us already

I have been getting
Yelling in my head

I have been loving badly
Again

America in Love, with Canada (II)

If the win isn't yours
truly or you mine,

we play with our food
and eat our words.

Not to make
such objects otherwise

but in service of making
this plane mean,

my meaning plain.
We walked around.

We benched ourselves
while the infrastructure

threatened lightly. Only I
can reach you now,

my chin on your shoulder
before the image. Rows

of sunbathers in coats
wore round sunglasses

on the High Line.
We faced them

more than each other:
reflection may have

non-relational qualities.
I can't go without you.

The Displaced City Poem Makes Love

When the rain starts, I step out
to stand in the stairwell

by the defunct kitchen entrance. I wait
to see the funeral home parking lot

turn entirely wet, for the pale
dry patches to brim and shine. Several

flashes rush the sky, fluorescing
blue behind the brick

Victorian, its gables and dormers
comically eerie. This makes twice

I've stood out here today; earlier
I watched the sun fade. As the rain

picks up, I listen. I'm hoping
it will come down harder. Once

upon a time I was looking at
a river in a rainstorm. A high rise

had us tucked beneath its girth
along the path connecting development

to development. How can I be
this small, this measured

by weather or company? All waterfronts
receive such things—first the foundation

and then the tower. Would I wish for
the rain without the building? And how dare

I put rain in a poem. How dare you
rise from nowhere and ruin the view.

The Blind Leading the Blind

I lack
the libido to write city

poems, writes Cam, and he professes
to like New Haven, smiling up

at the architectural
pastiche

and carrying my groceries home.
We lie horizontal

between the two,
the properly

Gothic
and its New

England imitation. Which part
is the libido

and which part
the city, which part the poem

and which part the lack?
We hardly

breathe for the mere
hours at hand. Nothing happens

here, except this address:
the I to the page, proper

noun to proper
noun, the eye-to-eye

losing that might begin
now or now.

The Worst Kind of New Yorker Imaginable

What is the meaning
of this New

Haven, from Middle English
from Old English from

Proto-Germanic, compare
Dutch or German

or Norwegian/Danish,
compare Middle Low German

perhaps in the sense of
Old Norse

heaving sea
or uplift, elevation

derived from Proto-
Indo-European

compare Old Irish
harbor, recess

a place of
safety, an anchorage

protected from the sea
was all I wanted

my familiar ire
mistaken for wanderlust

the buck of worldliness
stops there

in this town that could
have been any

-where, one can name
any place New

when one leaves behind
another Place

from the Middle Definition
of Proto-Semiotics

turning on signs
composing New Haven:

Let us help you study
for your final exams

says the church
letter board

Please curve
your dog

(curve
is underlined)

I'm on the lookout
for lighthouses

at the top of the park
at the base of the monument

I can see Long
Island from here

goddammit, and
compared to what?

Havens

havens, (gen.), haventis ADJ [XXXCW]
willing, eager, anxious; covetous;
———William Whitaker's WORDS

I'm no good at this: I cite you
jealously, coveting

every city, all your poems
and pronouns, subject

-hoods and libidinal
latitudes. I'm not so laissez-

faire as that, or am I?
To do or *ne fais pas*

when moving from the city
to the hamlet, or vice

versed in best intentions.
The church has changed

its sign, and I must inform you:
Opportunity knocks once

but temptation
leans on the bell

(enjambment original
though the sign is in all-caps).

I swear to God
I'd never have you

if it meant I could keep you,
but even that's a line

I'd feed you, if only
to steal it back.

"Living Without God is Like Trying to Dribble a Football"

for Colin Young

Do not punish me.
I have already punished
myself enough. I can do

only two kinds of work—
penance and vengeance.
I believe in little

but the coordination
between hand and eye
which falters and falters

not only on the field.
Where the leather narrows
to a point, I tried

to impale myself.
Where the letters narrow
to a point, I tried

and tried. No one
was dead yet.
I lived without

skill, sans team.
Even my enemies
tackled me lovingly.

Cam, Madison Square Park, June 2017

I lack the libido
to write city poems

writes Cam
and every time

I sit with him
I think but don't

say the words
because I lack

the poems
to revise the story

and I must leave the city
he cannot write of

and must capably
negate the lack

of other cities
which contain him

until finally all
I can do with what

is between us
is what passes

for a city
poem

if in name
alone

and I am left
with its failure

to think
but not say

though it pretends to lack
the words to be

a poem
of a different kind

which would tell
my dear friend

I am losing
these days of ours

but I lack nothing

Acknowledgements

Grateful acknowledgment is made to *Rattle Poets Respond* for publishing 'Graduate Student, Age 27, with a History of Sexual Harassment by Professors and Employers, Attends a Poetry Reading Four Days After the Tax Heist, Falling for a Man Who Isn't Her Lover, Temperature 54° F, New Haven, CT, December 5, 2017.'

Many thanks to all at **ignition**press for their careful attention to this pamphlet.

A special thanks to Joseph Harms, who saw me through the transition from New York City to New Haven.